Trains

Paul Stickland

MATHEW PRICE LIMITED

Old trains are pulled by steam engines.

They carry coal to burn in their fireboxes.

This is a STEAM TRAIN. These were the first sort of trains. They use coal in a firebox to heat up water until it turns to steam. The steam is forced through powerful pistons to give the engine the power to drive the wheels.

Steam trains are still in use all over the world, although most have been replaced by diesel or electric trains.

Steam engines can run on wood if there is no coal available.

The WAGON behind the engine is full of coal, which the fireman has to shovel into the firebox.

BRASS WHISTLES, which use steam to make a loud toot!

The smoke comes from the coal fire and escapes through the FUNNEL.

ENGINE NUMBER

WARNING LIGHTS

WARNING BELL

HOOK to connect carriages or wagons.

BUFFERS are often attached to hydraulic shock absorbers.

PISTONS drive the wheels. Safety valves regulate the steam pressure.

BOGIES have smaller wheels that guide the train round bends in the line.

This is one of the earliest steam engines in America. The red pusher at the front is called a cow-catcher.

A tram is like a bus: it runs through the town on rails set into the roads.

This American SMALL CAPS STEAM ENGINE is nearly one hundred years old. Trains like this helped settlers to spread across the country. They would deliver all the things the settlers would need, from house kits to food and even the mail.

CHIMNEY – shaped to catch sparks.

WARNING BELL

SAFETY VALVE

The native American Indians called these steam engines 'Iron Horses' when they first appeared.

The OIL LIGHT was probably fuelled by whale oil.

COW-CATCHER

TRAMS *usually get their electric power from overhead wires, which follow the rails. The conductor on the roof picks up the power and transfers it to the electric motors on the wheels.*

AUTOMATIC DOORS *are controlled by the driver.*

ROUTE NUMBER

TRAM NUMBER

A tram like this can carry about a hundred people. Imagine how crowded the roads would be if each of those people drove a car instead.

CARS *use the same road as trams.*

Four very powerful diesel-electric engines join

together to pull a hundred heavy coal trucks.

Powerful horns and lights warn people and animals that the Coal Train *is moving.*

Ventilation Grilles

The big blade on the front is to push branches or even animals off the tracks. It's a modern cow-catcher.

Blade

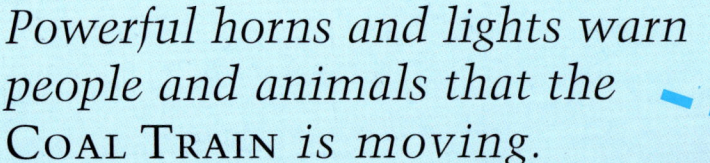

Trains are a very important way to transport enormous quantities of materials over huge distances. This one is taking coal straight from the coal mine where it is dug, and shifting it to the power station where it will be turned into electricity.

DIESEL ENGINES *are very powerful. Huge generators use diesel fuel to make electricity. Electricity powers the many engines connected to the wheels.*

The steel rails on which the train runs have to be very strong. So do the bridges, which have to cross great rivers and valleys.

Each of these COAL WAGONS *weighs one hundred tons, so the combined weight is immense. This is why four engines are needed to pull the train.*

STEPS *for the driver.*

This mountain train is climbing high into the mountains through the slippery ice and snow.

This is one of the fastest trains in the world.
It can travel at 180 miles an hour.

This MOUNTAIN TRAIN is designed to be able to climb the steep slopes in mountainous areas, where normal trains would not be able to work.

The train gets the power it needs for its electrical motors from overhead wires.

IRON TEETH

This is what makes this train special: a cog under the engine hooks on to these iron teeth and pulls the train up the mountain. The train is able to climb steep slopes in icy conditions where normal trains would slip. Why are these people travelling up this mountain?

This famous French passenger express is called the TGV (train de grande vitesse). The shape is specially streamlined to help it slice through the air, in order to achieve its high speeds.

Streamlined Shape

The track must be very very smooth or the train will jump off the rails at high speeds.

Shunting engine

Milk tanker

Tractor wagon

Coal wagon

Grain truck

Oil tanker

A small DIESEL SHUNTING ENGINE, *used for moving trucks short distances around the railyard.*

A TANKER *can hold any liquid, anything that flows – even flour and cement.*

LADDER

It is often easier and cheaper to deliver goods by rail.

Big vehicles and machinery are transported on open wagons like this; livestock and smaller items travel in covered wagons or container wagons.

An old-fashioned wooden COAL WAGON – nowadays these are made of metal and much larger.

A GRAIN TRUCK lets the contents flow from the bottom into containers below the track.

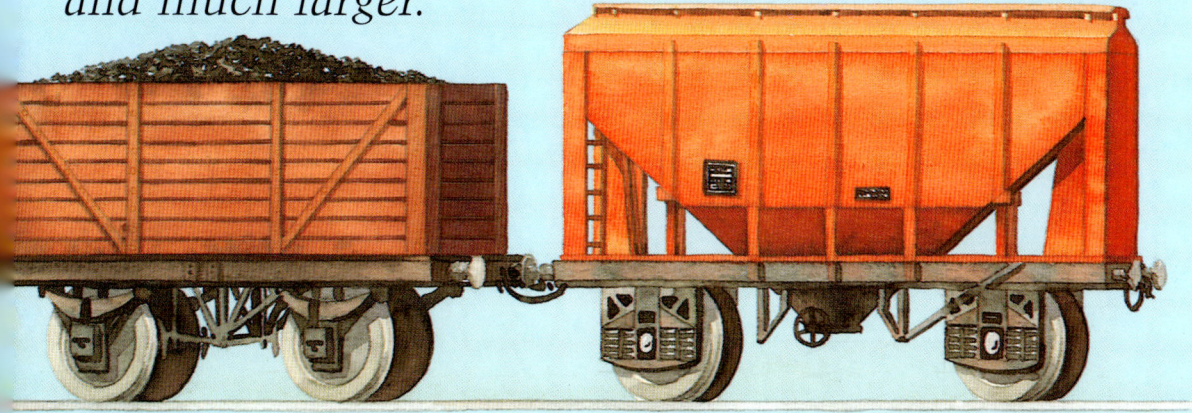

Eight wheels are needed on this TANKER to take the heavy weight. Four wheels at each end are mounted on swivelling bogies. This container holds thousands of gallons of oil.

The How, Why, What For Page

What sort of materials could these wagons be transporting?

What is a tank engine used for?

What would an electric engine be pulling?

Why are these cars on a train?

Where is this?

The Answers Page

 The open-topped wagon on the left could be carrying coal or wood.

 An electric engine is handy for pulling carriages or goods wagons.

 The wagon on the right has an outlet at the bottom: it could be transporting grain.

 The cars are being transported by train so only one driver is needed – the train driver.

 A tank engine is used to shunt wagons.

 A platform at a railway station.

Copyright © Paul Stickland 1991, 2004

This edition first published in the UK 2004
by Mathew Price Limited
The Old Glove Factory, Bristol Road
Sherborne, Dorset DT9 4HP, UK

Designed by Douglas Martin
All rights reserved
Printed in China
ISBN 1-84248-117-7